Unsung Heroes

RISK TAKERS

Heather E. Schwartz

Publishing Credits

Rachelle Cracchiolo, M.S.Ed., *Publisher*
Conni Medina, M.A.Ed., *Managing Editor*
Nika Fabienke, Ed.D., *Series Developer*
June Kikuchi, *Content Director*
Michelle Jovin, M.A., *Associate Editor*
Kevin Pham, *Graphic Designer*

The TIME logo is a registered trademark of TIME Inc. Used under license.

Image Credits: inside back cover Kazlova Iryna/Shutterstock; p.6 Vikram Raghuvanshi/iStock; p.7 Ennaimi Mouhssine/SIPA/Newscom; p.8 Xinhua/Alamy; p.9 AP Photo/Anil Dixit; p.13, pp.14–15, p.20 Public Domain; pp.16–17 European/FPG/Getty Images; pp. 18–19 ITAR-TASS Photo Agency/Alamy; p.19 (insert) Heritage Image Partnership Ltd/Alamy; pp.22–23 Granger Academic; p.24 Sergey Kohl/Shutterstock; p.25 GraphicaArtis/Bridgeman Images; pp.26-28, p.33 John van Hasselt/Sygma via Getty Images; p.29 Roman Tiraspolsky/Shutterstock; p.30 BLLF/John van Hasselt/Sygma via Getty Images; pp.36–37 Richard Levine/Alamy; p.39 Mark Schmidt, University at Albany; p.40 (top) Carol Guzy/Zuma Press/Newscom; p.41 Fabio Devilla/Shutterstock; p.48 Anthony Correia/Shutterstock; all other images from iStock and/or Shutterstock.

Teacher Created Materials

5301 Oceanus Drive
Huntington Beach, CA 92649-1030
www.tcmpub.com

ISBN 978-1-4258-5009-8

© 2019 Teacher Created Materials, Inc.
Printed in China
Nordica.072018.CA21800712

Table of Contents

Heroism in Action

Throughout history, heroes have risen to help others in times of war, tragedy, and **injustice**. Young and old, male and female, weak and strong, they've risked their lives. Some have even lost their lives, selflessly sacrificing everything for people in need.

But how many heroes do people really know about? There are a few famous names that come to mind immediately. Others are celebrated only briefly, the stories of their bravery and sacrifices quickly forgotten.

THINK LINK

> What traits make someone a hero?

> Who are the heroes in your life, and what makes them your heroes?

> How might people's lives change when they are labeled as heroes?

These are the stories of just a few unsung heroes throughout history. These six men, women, and children took action without expecting anything in return. Recognized or not, their heroism made a difference, and they deserve to have their stories told and remembered.

Real-Life Inspiration

Two teenage boys created Superman, the comic book hero, in the 1930s. One of them had lost his father, who was shot during a robbery. The tragedy may have inspired the boy to invent a hero who could survive anything.

The Girl Who Refused to Marry

Rekha Kalindi (REH-kuh kaw-LIN-dee) was only 11 years old when she risked everything to take control of the course of the rest of her life.

Growing up in a poor village in India, Kalindi started working to help support her family when she was only 4 years old. She was about 9 when she finally began attending a special school for local village children. Kalindi loved learning and did well in her classes. She knew that if she could get a good education, she had a chance to break free from her family's state of **poverty**.

However, when Kalindi was 11 years old, her world came crashing down around her—Kalindi's parents told her she would have to stop going to school. They had decided to arrange a marriage for their daughter.

Lost Chance to Learn

The law says that Indian children between ages 6 and 14 must attend school. But millions of families do not follow the law. Parents need their kids to work and earn money for the family.

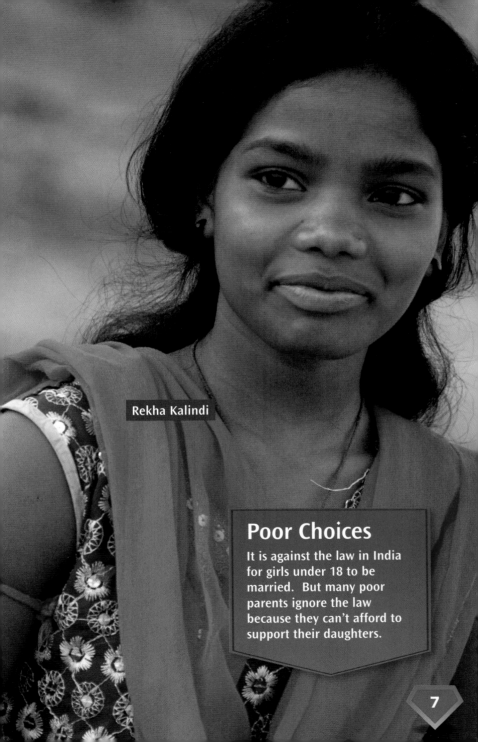

Rekha Kalindi

Poor Choices

It is against the law in India for girls under 18 to be married. But many poor parents ignore the law because they can't afford to support their daughters.

People protest child marriage in India in 2015.

A Matter of Life and Death

When girls marry before they turn 15, they often give birth before their bodies are ready. These child brides are five times more likely to die in childbirth than older women.

Kalindi knew many girls who had married at her age, but she didn't want to be one of them. In fact, Kalindi's own sister was married when she was 11 years old, and after four **miscarriages**, she was told she couldn't have children. Kalindi didn't want to suffer the same fate, and she didn't want to leave school.

Kalindi later said that when she refused to marry, her mother beat her and withheld food from her, telling Kalindi that parents had the right to make decisions for their children. But Kalindi had learned at school that she was not a piece of property. She reached out to her school for help. Teachers, classmates, and even a government official got involved, and eventually, Kalindi's parents allowed her to remain unmarried and return to school.

After that, Kalindi spoke publicly against child marriage. She convinced many adults in her village, including her own mother, that it was wrong. Kalindi's refusal to marry gave her power, and she used it to work toward stopping a terrible tradition in her country.

Beyond India

Child marriage is not just in India. In the United States, 27 states have no minimum age laws for marriage. Hundreds of thousands of underage marriages took place in the United States between 2000 and 2010. Children as young as 12 years old were married in Alaska, Louisiana, and South Carolina in that time.

Child Marriages in the United States

Between 2000 and 2010, it is estimated that there were nearly 250,000 people married in the United States who were 17 years old or younger. The map shows the minimum legal age for marriage in each state. Over half of the states have no law regarding the minimum age for marriage.

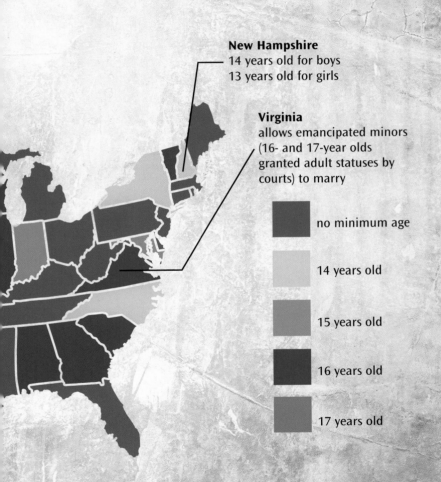

New Hampshire
14 years old for boys
13 years old for girls

Virginia
allows emancipated minors
(16- and 17-year olds
granted adult statuses by
courts) to marry

no minimum age

14 years old

15 years old

16 years old

17 years old

Source: Tahirih Justice Center and the *New York Times*

The Priest Who Chose Moloka'i

Jozef de Veuster (YOH-zehf duh vuh-STEHR) was born in Belgium in 1840. As a young man, he went to Hawai'i, became a priest, and changed his name to Father Damien. While working in Hawai'i, he learned about the island of Moloka'i (mah-luh-KIGH), where people were sent when they showed signs of the contagious Hansen's disease (also known as leprosy). These people were **quarantined** on the island so they wouldn't spread the disease to the rest of society. They became known as *lepers* (LEH-puhrs), and the term took on an offensive meaning.

Father Damien felt called to help the people living on Moloka'i. He went to the island, determined to live among them and work with them, despite the fact that he was putting himself in danger of catching the disease.

Hansen's Disease Today

Hansen's disease causes **disfiguration** and nerve damage. It is contagious, but it is not easy to catch. Medicine has been available to cure the disease since 1995.

Father Damien sits with a group of people with Hansen's disease on Molokaʻi.

Banished

King Kamehameha V (kuh-MAY-uh-MAY-huh) ruled Hawaiʻi from 1863 to 1872. In 1865, he said that anyone with Hansen's disease must be **exiled** to live apart from the rest of society. The law was not lifted for more than a hundred years.

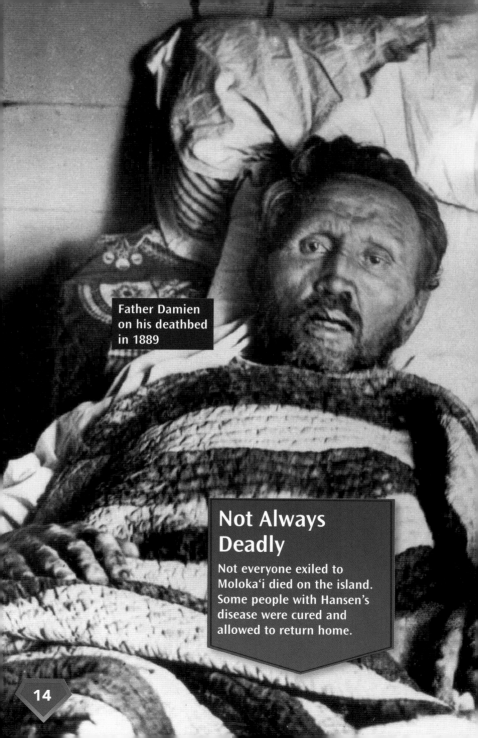

Father Damien
on his deathbed
in 1889

Not Always Deadly

Not everyone exiled to
Moloka'i died on the island.
Some people with Hansen's
disease were cured and
allowed to return home.

People with Hansen's disease were sent to die on Moloka'i. However, Father Damien refused to give up on them and instead focused his efforts on the time they had left to live. Father Damien organized the patients on Moloka'i to build houses and a water system and start their own schools. He also helped them put together bands and choirs to play music, sing, and entertain the island residents.

The community that Father Damien built was his own as much as it was the patients'. He lived on the island for 12 years, and when he **contracted** Hansen's disease himself, he accepted it as God's will. Father Damien had bandaged patients' open sores without rushing to wash his hands. He had shared food with them, never treating them as people who were dirty or contaminated. Father Damien died in 1889 on Moloka'i. He was **canonized** as a saint in the Roman Catholic Church in 2009.

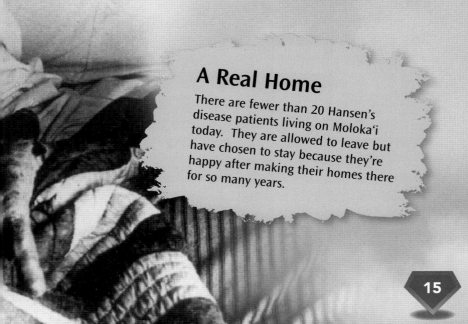

A Real Home

There are fewer than 20 Hansen's disease patients living on Moloka'i today. They are allowed to leave but have chosen to stay because they're happy after making their homes there for so many years.

A group of Jewish people wait in line in Poland for food from the Red Cross.

The Doctor Who Faked an Epidemic

Dr. Eugene Lazowski (yoo-JEEN luh-ZOW-skee) was serving in the Polish army when German soldiers invaded his country in 1939. Lazowski was sent to work for the Polish Red Cross, but he was not allowed to treat Jewish people by order of the **Nazis**. If he did—and the Nazis found out about it—Lazowski would be sentenced to death.

As a doctor, Lazowski felt he should help anyone who needed his care, regardless of religion. So, instead of obeying German orders, he did what he knew was right. Lazowski worked out a secret system to help Jewish neighbors living in a **ghetto** behind his house. If a Jewish person hung a rag on his or her fence, Lazowski would know that he or she needed him to make a house call during the night.

Based in Hate

Adolf Hitler was the leader of the Nazi Party. The Nazis aimed to create a "master race" by **exterminating** Jewish people around the world. The Nazis also went after homosexuals, non-Christians, and anyone else they felt was **inferior**.

Death Toll

When Germany invaded Poland in 1939, Great Britain and France declared war. It was the start of World War II, which would not end until 1945. In that time, more than 40 million people died from the effects of war.

female prisoners at Auschwitz-Birkenau concentration camp in Poland, the deadliest camp

Lazowski tried to help his neighbors by treating their illnesses. Soon, they faced an even greater danger. The Nazis had begun rounding up Jewish people and sending them to work in concentration camps, where they faced hard labor, starvation, and even death.

It wasn't easy for Jewish people to avoid the camps, but illness was one possible way out. The Nazis were fearful of an **epidemic**. Typhus, a disease that spread quickly in places where people were crowded together in unsanitary conditions, was to be avoided at all costs. The disease was deadly and could easily infect soldiers, too. So, Jewish people who tested positive for epidemic typhus were kept out of the camps.

Knowing this, Lazowski was in an unusual position for a doctor. Normally, he wanted to cure patients, but now, they might be better off sick.

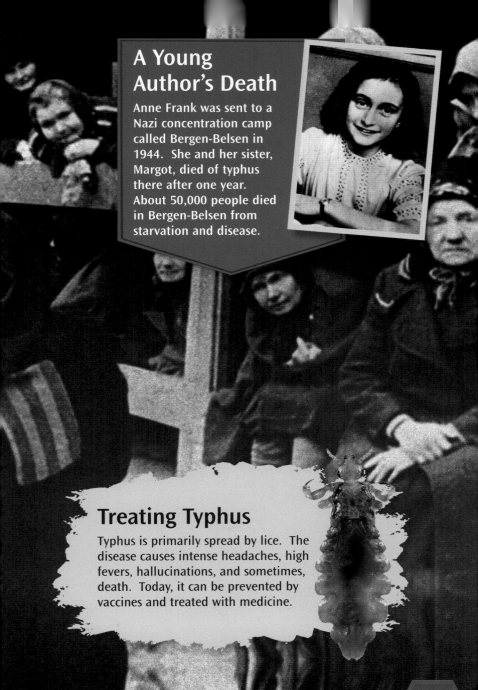

A Young Author's Death

Anne Frank was sent to a Nazi concentration camp called Bergen-Belsen in 1944. She and her sister, Margot, died of typhus there after one year. About 50,000 people died in Bergen-Belsen from starvation and disease.

Treating Typhus

Typhus is primarily spread by lice. The disease causes intense headaches, high fevers, hallucinations, and sometimes, death. Today, it can be prevented by vaccines and treated with medicine.

Dr. Eugene Lazowski

Millions Dead

In 1939 (the start of World War II), there were 9.5 million Jewish people living in Europe. In 1945 (the end of the war), that number had dropped to just 3.8 million. Nearly half of the approximately 6 million Jewish people who died in the war were killed from poisonous gas or from being shot.

Lazowski knew another doctor named Stanislaw Matulewicz (STAN-ih-slahv muh-TOO-luh-vich) who discovered something interesting about typhus. Matulewicz had found that when people were injected with a certain strain of typhus, they would test positive for the disease. However, the patients would not actually contract the disease or suffer from it in any way.

Injecting only Jewish people with the strain of typhus would not save them. The Nazis would instead kill them right away. But Lazowski knew he could fake an epidemic by injecting people who were not Jewish as well. When enough people tested positive for typhus, the Nazis announced a quarantine. The quarantine was placed over an area where about eight thousand Jewish and non-Jewish people lived.

No one was allowed to leave the quarantined area. Nazis would not go there for fear of contracting the disease. Lazowski's actions saved the lives of thousands of people who would otherwise have gone to concentration camps.

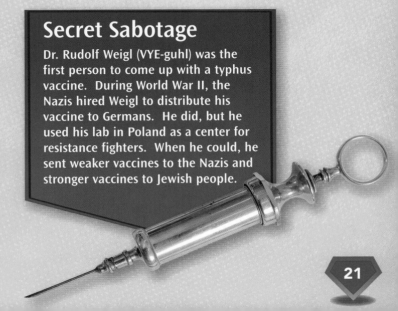

Secret Sabotage

Dr. Rudolf Weigl (VYE-guhl) was the first person to come up with a typhus vaccine. During World War II, the Nazis hired Weigl to distribute his vaccine to Germans. He did, but he used his lab in Poland as a center for resistance fighters. When he could, he sent weaker vaccines to the Nazis and stronger vaccines to Jewish people.

The Teen Who Saved a Country

Sybil Ludington was born in Connecticut in 1761. During the American Revolution, her father, a colonel, led a **regiment** of American patriots.

One night in 1777, a man came to the Ludingtons' house with a warning. British soldiers had attacked and were burning Danbury, a nearby town. Danbury was where the **munitions** were kept for the entire region. If Danbury was conquered, the region would have a hard time resisting the British.

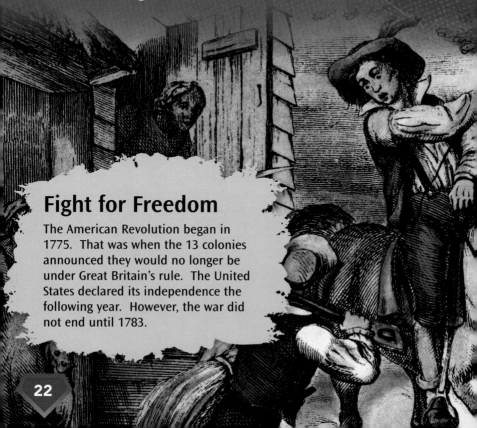

Fight for Freedom

The American Revolution began in 1775. That was when the 13 colonies announced they would no longer be under Great Britain's rule. The United States declared its independence the following year. However, the war did not end until 1783.

The colonel's regiment was needed for battle, but it was planting season and the soldiers had gone home to work their farms. Someone would have to ride a horse to each farm, tell the soldiers of the situation, and gather them for a fight against the British.

There was, however, one huge problem—the rider who'd come to the Ludingtons' home was too exhausted to go any farther. And Colonel Ludington could not make the trip either. He had to prepare for the battle himself. *Someone* had to save Danbury, or the fight would be lost.

Doing Their Part

Many teenage girls sewed uniforms and managed farms during the American Revolution. They were not allowed to serve in the armed forces. However, at least one girl (16-year-old Deborah Samson) dressed as a boy and joined the military to fight the British.

At 16, Ludington was her father's oldest child. Historians are unsure whether the colonel asked her to make the trip or whether she offered to go. Either way, Ludington set out to warn the soldiers and gather them for battle.

Ludington rode to each soldier's farm, spreading the news. By the end of her trip, she'd ridden about 40 miles (65 kilometers) through the night. By morning, the regiment was ready to battle at Danbury.

The British soldiers greatly outnumbered the American patriots at Danbury. The patriots could not save the town from being burned and **ransacked**, but they held their positions and eventually forced the British to withdraw. After the battle, George Washington—the future first president of the United States—stopped by the Ludingtons' house. He thanked Ludington personally for her bravery and heroism.

Not Forgotten

In 1975, the U.S. Postal Service honored Sybil Ludington by putting her on a stamp. There are also historical markers along the route of her ride. A statue of Ludington stands in Carmel, New York.

Midnight Rider

Paul Revere is famous for a similar heroic act when he rode 14 mi. (22.5 km) to warn patriots of a British attack in Massachusetts. While he is often described as shouting, "The British are coming!" Revere did not actually yell anything. Instead, he tried to ride as quietly as possible so as not to be heard by the British soldiers.

Revere on his famous night ride

The Boy Who Broke Free

When Iqbal Masih (IHK-bahl ma-SEE) was four years old, his mother needed an operation. Unfortunately, Masih's family could not afford to pay for it, so his mother made an arrangement common to many **impoverished** families in Pakistan—she sold Masih into bonded labor. That meant he could not return home until his mother's **debt** was paid. On his fifth birthday, Masih was taken away to work in a carpet factory.

At the factory, Masih was treated very poorly. He sat hunched at a carpet **loom** for 12 hours each day with few breaks, he was underfed, and his boss often beat him. Sometimes, Masih's boss chained him to the loom so he could not escape. Earning just pennies each day, the child had no hope of paying back his mother's debt and earning his freedom.

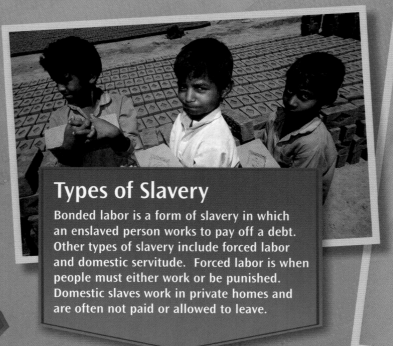

Types of Slavery

Bonded labor is a form of slavery in which an enslaved person works to pay off a debt. Other types of slavery include forced labor and domestic servitude. Forced labor is when people must either work or be punished. Domestic slaves work in private homes and are often not paid or allowed to leave.

Adding to the Debt

The original debt that Masih had to pay off was the equivalent of about $12, which he could have paid off in about a month. However, his mother later added to the debt when she borrowed money to pay for a wedding feast for Masih's half-brother. After that, Masih's debt jumped to $250.

Iqbal Masih

Ignoring the Law

In 1992, a law was passed in Pakistan that made it illegal for children younger than 14 to work. However, many companies did not follow the law. Today, there are still about 20 million children working in Pakistan.

Pakistani children work at a carpet loom.

Masih spent the next five years working in **captivity**. Then one day, when he was 10 years old, Masih saw a poster in the village that said slave labor was illegal in Pakistan. The poster included information about how to contact the Bonded Labour Liberation Front (BLLF)—an organization that helps to free child workers and enslaved people in Pakistan.

Masih managed to contact the BLLF without his boss at the carpet factory finding out. **Activists** came to the factory to rescue him and hundreds of other children. By then, Masih was in poor health; he was wheezing and **frail** and much smaller than he should have been for his age. However, none of that mattered much to Masih—he was finally free.

Modern-Day Slavery

The United Nations (UN) estimates that almost 21 million people are forced to work against their wills. There are enslaved people all over the world, including in the United States.

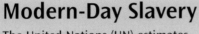

Masih did not fade quietly into regular life after he was set free. Instead, he attended school and became an activist for his cause. He spoke against the horrors he had **endured** and witnessed. Masih even traveled to Sweden and the United States where he told people what was really happening in the carpet industry and how child workers were treated.

Masih's words impacted many people. He received a Reebok Youth in Action Award in 1994. More importantly, he was credited with helping children by making a difference in the carpet industry. Stores and customers refused to purchase carpets made by enslaved children. Dozens of Pakistani factories shut down.

Big Dreams

The Reebok Youth in Action Award gave Masih $15,000 (about $25,000 today). He said he would use the money to go to school so he could be a lawyer. Brandeis University, in Massachusetts, also offered to pay for him to go to their college.

Masih celebrates winning the Reebok Youth in Action Award.

Even though Masih fought to end child labor, there are still children around the world who are forced to work long hours in sometimes hazardous jobs.

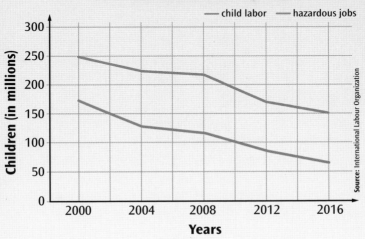

5–15 Year Olds Working

— child labor — hazardous jobs

Children (in millions)

300
250
200
150
100
50
0

2000   2004   2008   2012   2016

Years

Source: International Labour Organization

> The graph doesn't explain what types of jobs are considered "hazardous" for children. What do you consider a hazardous job for someone under 15 years old?

> What comparisons can you make between the amount of children working overall and the amount working in hazardous jobs from 2000 to 2016?

> Based on the data in the graph, what predictions can you make about the number of children working and the number of children working in hazardous jobs for 2020 and beyond?

31

Every time carpet-factory owners reported **losses**, Masih and other enslaved children counted it as a win. However, powerful people in the carpet industry were not about to let Masih get away with **undermining** them. Soon, Masih began to receive death threats.

On April 16, 1995, Masih set out on a bike ride with his cousins to deliver dinner to his uncle, who was out watering his fields. When the boys got about halfway there, they heard two gunshots. The boys saw Masih fall off his bike; he had been shot. At just 12 years old, Iqbal Masih had been murdered.

Authorities could not prove the murder was tied to his activism, but many people believed he was killed for speaking out. After the shooting, the Pakistan Carpet Manufacturers and Exporters Association reported a $10 million loss in orders. Even after his death, Masih was an activist and a hero. He gave everything he had to improve life for child slaves in Pakistan.

Biggest Business

The United States is the largest **importer** of carpets from Pakistan. People in the United States purchased $42 million worth of carpets from Pakistan in 1994, the year before Masih's death. After Masih's death, the number of imports from Pakistan dropped sharply.

Masih's mother holds a picture of her son as people mourn his death.

In His Honor

In 2000, Masih received the first World's Children's Prize. The winner of this award is chosen by millions of children each year. The **posthumous** award was given to Masih to honor his work helping enslaved children.

The Cop Who Saved Hundreds

On September 11, 2001, an airplane crashed into the North Tower of the World Trade Center, in New York City. Terri Tobin, a lieutenant with the New York City Police Department, arrived just moments after the plane crashed. As the sky filled with ash from the burning building, Tobin grabbed a strong, bulletproof helmet and set about helping people. Moments later, she was horrified to watch a second plane strike the South Tower.

The Towers

The World Trade Center towers were key landmarks of the New York City skyline. The iconic towers were 1,360 feet (415 meters) tall. The towers were attacked once before, in 1993, when terrorists bombed the World Trade Center. That attack killed six people and caused considerable damage, but it did not bring down the towers.

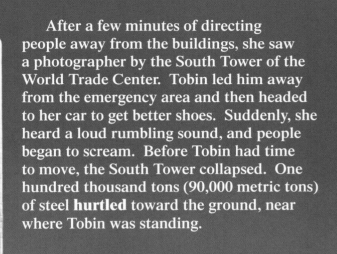

After a few minutes of directing people away from the buildings, she saw a photographer by the South Tower of the World Trade Center. Tobin led him away from the emergency area and then headed to her car to get better shoes. Suddenly, she heard a loud rumbling sound, and people began to scream. Before Tobin had time to move, the South Tower collapsed. One hundred thousand tons (90,000 metric tons) of steel **hurtled** toward the ground, near where Tobin was standing.

No Mistake

Tobin, like many other Americans, initially thought the plane crashes were some horrible accident. When the second plane hit the South Tower, she knew it was a terrorist attack. Tobin and others would later learn that al-Qaeda (al-KY-duh) terrorists were behind the attacks.

The North Tower (left) was struck first, followed by the South Tower (right).

When the 110-floor building fell, the effect was like an explosion—it blasted Tobin out of her shoes and hurled her across a four-lane highway. Chunks of concrete landed on top of Tobin and buried her up to her waist. Her sturdy helmet was cracked in half, and when she reached her hand to the back of her skull, she felt something sticking out. A chunk of concrete had hit her head so hard that it had become **embedded** in her skull. In addition to her head wound, Tobin also had a bruised kidney and a broken ankle.

Despite her injuries, Tobin didn't spend much time worrying about herself. She let two emergency workers wrap the piece of concrete in her head so it would not fall out, before racing to join firefighters and paramedics helping others out of the wreckage. As she worked, the North Tower began to collapse. This time, Tobin attempted to run from the crash, but her injured ankle prevented her progress. Tobin felt something slam into her back (which she later learned was a windowpane), before she took cover in a nearby apartment building.

More Injuries

When Tobin went to get her head wrapped, the emergency workers also gave her saline solution to wash out her eyes and mouth. She swished the liquid and spit out what she thought was a chunk of concrete. It was only when she looked at the ground that Tobin discovered she had actually spit out a tooth.

First Responders

The New York City Police Department, Fire Department, and other emergency workers were some of the first to respond on 9/11. They ran into the towers and helped get people away from the crashing buildings. Together, they saved the lives of about 25,000 people in and around the World Trade Center.

First responders work to clear the wreckage of the World Trade Center after both towers collapsed.

When Tobin turned around, she discovered about a hundred horrified people **huddled** together in the apartment building. Tobin led the group to the lobby of the building, then opened a door to attract the attention of some of her co-workers. They were prepared to bring the people to safety, and they wanted to help Tobin, too. One offered to carry her to a boat. Not realizing she had glass sticking out of her back, Tobin said she was able to walk.

When she finally made it to a hospital in New Jersey, Tobin was given more difficult news—the doctors could not give her **anesthesia** due to her head injury. Doctors removed the chunk of concrete from Tobin's skull, wrapped her broken ankle, and gave her 80 stitches to close the wound in her back, all while Tobin remained awake. After just two months of rest, Tobin returned to her job at the police department. She said she was not done risking her life to save others.

Inspired to Serve

Heroes of 9/11 have inspired others to risk their lives the same way. Brittany Roy joined the New York City Police Department in 2017. Roy's father was a New York City police officer who was killed at the World Trade Center.

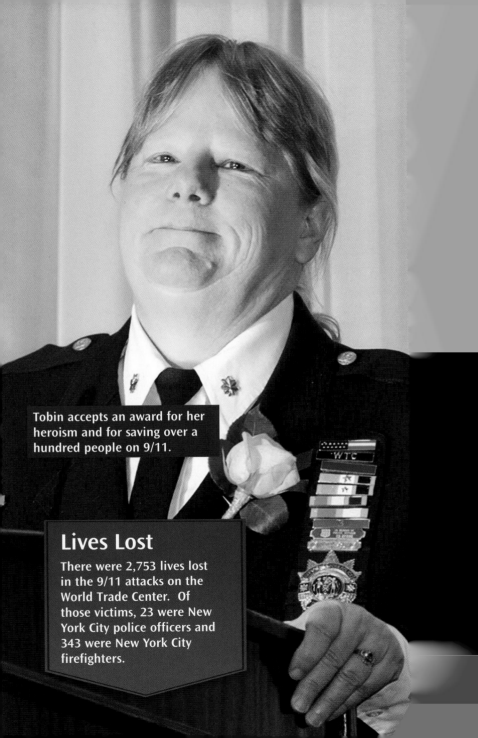

Tobin accepts an award for her heroism and for saving over a hundred people on 9/11.

Lives Lost

There were 2,753 lives lost in the 9/11 attacks on the World Trade Center. Of those victims, 23 were New York City police officers and 343 were New York City firefighters.

How to Be a Hero

In 2011, researchers performed a study of four thousand adults living in the United States. They found that 20 percent of those adults could be called heroes. They had stood up to injustice, stepped in to help strangers, or helped during major emergencies.

Inspiring Future Heroes

Heroes are people who demonstrate bravery in the face of danger without focusing on the fear they feel. Instead, they move forward in the direction of what they know is right, by helping others and acting in ways that support their deepest beliefs.

Heroes are often regular people who become heroes under specific circumstances. Some risk their health and safety during war and tragedy; others stand up to people who are harming others. In every tragedy, there are always heroes who take steps to support their beliefs and goals for a better tomorrow.

The more we know about heroes, the more we can learn from their powerful stories. We may even be inspired to follow in their footsteps and one day become the heroes others will read about.

Heroes Create Heroes

Witnessing a heroic act can lead to what some people call a *state of elevation*, in which a person feels calm and loved. This state of elevation leads people to perform their own heroic acts. That puts more witnesses in states of elevation, and leads them to perform heroic acts, too.

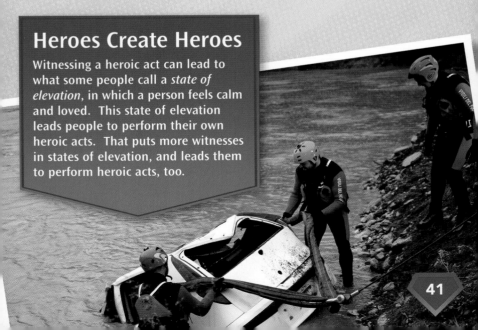

Glossary

activists—people who use strong actions to try to make changes in societies

anesthesia—a type of medicine that makes a person unconscious or causes a person to feel a numbness

authorities—people who have the power to make decisions and enforce laws or rules

canonized—officially declared a saint

captivity—the state of being kept in a certain place and not being allowed to leave or be free

contracted—became ill with a disease

debt—amount of money that is owed to a person, company, or bank

disfiguration—the state of an appearance being damaged by someone or something

embedded—placed or set something firmly into something else

endured —experienced suffering or pain for a long time

epidemic—a situation in which a disease spreads very quickly and affects a large number of people

exiled—forced to leave home and live somewhere else

exterminating—completely destroying or killing off a group of people or animals

frail—having less than a normal amount of strength

ghetto—a part of a city in which members of a particular group live, usually in poor conditions

huddled—gathered close together

hurtled—fell or moved with great speed and force

importer—someone or something who brings a product into a country to be sold

impoverished—someone who has little money or wealth

inferior—of less value or not as good

injustice—unfair treatment against a person or group

loom—a machine that is used to weave yarns or threads together to produce cloth

losses—decreases in amount of money

miscarriages—situations in which pregnancies end too early and do not result in the births of live babies

munitions—military equipment and supplies, especially weapons

Nazis—members of a German political party led by Adolf Hitler, which controlled Germany from 1933 to 1945

posthumous—happening or done after a person's death

poverty—the state of having little money

quarantined—kept away from others to prevent a disease from spreading

ransacked—searched a place in a way that caused damage or disorder

regiment—a military unit that is made up of several large groups of soldiers

undermining—making someone or something less effective or weaker in a secret way

Index

Check It Out!

Books

D'Adamo, Francesco. 2005. *Iqbal*. New York: Aladdin.

Zullo, Allan. 2015. *10 True Tales: Heroes of 9/11*. New York: Scholastic.

Videos

Liberty's Kids 121. 2002. *Sybil Ludington*. DIC Entertainment.

Halloran, Neil, dir. 2015. *The Fallen of World War II*. www.fallen.io/ww2/. Higher Media.

History. *9/11 Timeline*. www.history.com/topics/9-11-attacks/videos/911-timeline. A&E Television Networks, LLC.

Websites

Humanium. *Children's Rights Worldwide*. www.humanium.org/en/map-respect-children-rights-worldwide/.

National Park Service. *Father Damien*. www.nps.gov/kala/learn/historyculture/damien.htm.

The World's Children's Prize. *The World's Children's Prize Laureates*. www.worldschildrensprize.org/laureates.

Try It!

You don't have to have super powers to be considered a hero. Heroes are ordinary people who stand up for what they believe in.

- Choose one of your heroes. It can be someone you know or someone you have learned about. Imagine he or she is actually a comic book superhero.

- Draw a comic book about your hero.

- Be sure to include details about your hero, such as clothing, masks, form of transportation, etc.

- Give your hero a situation to overcome.

- Add dialogue.

- If you know your hero personally, give him or her the comic book. If you do not know your hero, share your comic book with friends to teach them more about your hero.

About the Author

Heather E. Schwartz has written more than 60 nonfiction books for children and teenagers. She lives in upstate New York with her husband, two young sons, and two cats. When she is not writing, she enjoys reading, singing, learning to play the ukulele, and performing with an improv theater troupe. She was in New York City when tragedy struck on September 11, 2001, and she is very grateful to all of the heroes who responded that day.